Skyrockets for the President

A true story about George Washington and his grandson

By FLORENCE LAUGHLIN
Illustrated by George Roth

RAND McNALLY & COMPANY

Chicago   New York   San Francisco

Library of Congress Cataloging in Publication Data

Laughlin, Florence.
  Skyrockets for the President.

  SUMMARY: Traces the expectations and fears of George Washington's young grandson before the first presidential inauguration.
  1. Washington, George, Pres. U.S., 1732-1799—Juvenile literature. 2. Custis, George Washington Parke, 1781-1857—Juvenile literature. [1. Washington, George, Pres. U.S., 1732-1799. 2. Custis, George Washington Parke, 1781-1857. 3. Presidents] I. Roth, George, 1932-   illus. II. Title.
E312.19.L38 1973   973.4'1'0924 [B] [920] 73-7710
ISBN 0-528-82550-X
ISBN 0-528-82551-8   (lib. bdg.)

TEXT: *Copyright © 1973 by Florence Laughlin*
ILLUSTRATIONS: *Copyright © 1973 by Rand McNally & Company*
All rights reserved
Printed in the United States of America by Rand McNally & Company

First printing 1973

*For three young Americans—
Nedra, Paul, and Trevor*

Skyrockets *for the* President

It was springtime at Mount Vernon, the home of General George Washington. A wild, sweet wind blew across the land. It slipped in through the window of the tiny octagon schoolhouse in the garden.

The children from the Big House were there, taking their lessons. The two girls bent busily over their copybooks. But Little Wash was staring out the window.

He was dreaming about his pony. Grandpapa had promised to take him riding over the plantation that day. Little Wash could think of nothing else.

"George Washington Parke Custis!"

Little Wash blinked and turned around. "Yes, sir, Mr. Lear," he said to the schoolmaster.

"What is the sum of seven and nine?"

Cousin Harriot looked up and giggled. And Little Wash found himself stammering.

"It—it is— The sum of seven and nine is—"

The problem was never to be answered. At that very moment—from somewhere outside—there arose such a racket *nobody* could think.

Sounds of angry shouts and pounding feet shook the air. Hens were squawking. Dogs were barking.

Little Wash jumped to his feet. His inkwell went flying through space as he ran to the door.

At his heels came Cousin Harriot and his sister Nelly. Even Mr. Lear dashed outside to see what was going on.

Everyone on the plantation seemed to be moving at once—all running pell-mell toward the kennels.

Far out in front—leaping over bushes, bounding through the grass—ran two of Grandpapa's great hounds. Vulcan had something in his mouth.

"Stop, thief!" shouted Fauncie the cook. "Drop that ham!"

Little Wash joined in the chase.

When they all reached the kennels the dogs were safely inside. The gate was closed. And gray-haired Billy Lee, Grandpapa's servant and friend, stood in front of it.

"No use bothering those hounds now," he said to the angry cook. "That old juicy ham is gone forever."

Little Wash could see the dogs through the fence. They crouched happily over the stolen food.

In a few minutes Grandmother appeared. She wore a big white apron and had a ruffled cap on her head. Her plump face grew pink when she heard what had happened.

"Your Grandpapa's hounds are a plague and a nuisance, Little Wash," she declared. "They bark at my parrot, they chase the pheasants, and they beg at the table. *They will simply have to go.*"

"Who will have to go, Patsy dear?" came a voice from behind her.

That was Grandpapa himself. He, too, had heard the commotion from his desk in the library of the Big House.

"Vulcan is in trouble again, Grandpapa," said Little Wash. His heart was beating very hard. "He stole a ham from the cookhouse—"

"Grabbed it from under my very nose," cried Fauncie.

"And I planned to have it for your dinner, Papa," said Grandmother in distress.

Little Wash was sure he saw Grandpapa smile.

"We'll make do with mutton and cheese again today," he said to his wife. "As for the hounds, Patsy dear—don't forget, they were a gift from a good

friend. Billy Lee will keep them in the kennels from now on. And Wash may take them for a run every day on the leash."

Little Wash laughed with relief. The big dogs had come to the fence, and he reached out to pet them. He loved them as much as Grandpapa did. When he was very small he used to ride them like ponies.

By now the plantation people were drifting back to their chores. But Grandpapa had not forgotten his promise.

"Are you ready to go riding with me now, Little Wash?" he asked. "Did you finish your lessons?"

Little Wash looked anxiously at Tobias Lear, who was standing nearby.

The schoolmaster smiled down at him. "I'll give the boy double the lessons tomorrow, General Washington," he promised.

More than anything else in the world Little Wash liked to go riding—especially when Grandpapa rode alongside on his big white stallion. The spirited little pony had to gallop to keep abreast of the big horse.

First they rode down to the pasture to see Nelson. Nelson was one of the horses Grandpapa rode during the Revolutionary War. He was very old now and whinnied softly as he came to greet them.

Grandpapa fed him a sugar lump from his pocket. Little Wash climbed on the gate to stroke his neck.

"He never flinched in battle," Grandpapa said proudly.

After that they rode past the deer park, where Little Wash saw a baby fawn. It was so new it tottered on its legs. "I wish I could touch it," he said longingly.

"It wouldn't be wise," Grandpapa replied. "The mother deer would be very nervous."

Little Wash looked back over his shoulder as they rode on toward the river. Just before they turned to go down to the wharf, he saw the doe nudge her fawn into the shadows among the trees.

The Mount Vernon farms stretched along the great Potomac River for as far as Little Wash could see. There were orchards of apple and peach and cherry and fields of corn and wheat. Some of the fields were not yet planted. Men were ploughing the rich, dark earth.

Grandpapa and Little Wash stopped at the wharf to watch the sailing ships go by. Workmen were loading a long barge with bales of hides and boxes of biscuit—all made on the plantation, all going to faraway places.

The men looked up from their work to smile and wave at the big man in the tricorn hat, mounted beside his son.

Little Wash wasn't Grandpapa's real son, of course. General Washington had no children of his

own. Wash was Martha Washington's grandson. He and his sister Nelly had lived at Mount Vernon since shortly after they were born. Grandpapa had adopted them after their father died.

Now Grandpapa went to chat with the men and to ask about their families. Little Wash climbed among the bales and boxes and wondered what it would be like to ride on the barge all the way to the sea.

"Time to turn back, Little Wash," said Grandpapa finally. He took his big watch from his waistcoat pocket and snapped it open. "It's half after two. I've just time to get home and have my hair powdered for dinner."

Grandpapa always ate promptly at three o'clock.

"Mutton and cheese again," he muttered as he turned the white stallion around. "Thanks to those greedy hounds."

Little Wash laughed.

"I'll race you home, Grandpapa," he cried. He kicked his heels, and his pony galloped swiftly ahead toward the great white house on the hill.

One day a visitor came to Mount Vernon. Little Wash was in his favorite place—the turret room atop the Big House. From there he could see in every

direction. He saw Grandpapa making his rounds of the farm. And he saw the stranger come riding through the plantation gates and up the serpentine drive.

When Little Wash hurried downstairs he found Grandmother, Nelly, and Cousin Harriot in the lower hallway. They were just greeting the visitor.

Grandmother looked fondly at her grandson. "Little Wash," she said. "This is Mr. Charles Thomson."

Little Wash bowed politely.

"Mr. Thomson has come all the way from New York to bring a message for Grandpapa."

"I rode night and day to see the General," said the man smiling down at the boy. "And I find him not in."

"He's coming now, sir," said Little Wash eagerly. "I saw him riding past the old mill."

While Grandmother led the visitor to the sitting room, Little Wash and Nelly ran outside to wait for Grandpapa.

"I wonder what Mr. Thomson's message can be,"

said Nelly. "It must be an important one."

"I don't know," said Little Wash. "But he came through the gates in an awful hurry."

Not until later did they learn the surprising news.

When Little Wash came down to dinner, the family was already at table in the big dining room. The visitor from New York was seated next to Grandpapa.

Little Wash slipped quietly into his chair, hoping nobody would notice that he was late.

Nobody did. In fact, Grandpapa didn't seem to see him at all. He looked solemn. And Grandmother's usually happy face was almost sad!

"What's the matter, Grandmother?" asked Wash.

Before she could answer his question the visitor spoke up. "Nothing is the *matter,* young man," he said in a booming voice. "I bring great news to this house. General Washington has been elected President of the United States."

President. Little Wash looked questioningly around the table. He wasn't quite sure what that meant. But he knew it must be something important for Grandpapa to look so serious.

"Does it mean you'll have to go away, Grandpapa?" asked Nelly. Her dark eyes were troubled.

Grandpapa nodded. "I'm afraid so, Nelly dear," he said. "Our government is far away in New York town, and that is where the president must live. It grieves me to leave this house that we all love so much. But if my country needs me I cannot refuse to go."

Then Grandmother smiled and made everything all right again, as she always did.

"Don't look so woeful, my children," she said gently. "Grandpapa can't get away from us that easily. He must leave in a few days to take the Oath of Office. But as soon as we are packed and ready we will follow in the carriage."

At that, Little Wash felt better. And he turned with a will to the bowl of savory soup that was set before him.

With the coming of Mr. Thomson the quiet life at Mount Vernon turned topsy-turvy. People came from all around the countryside to honor the man who was to be the first president and to wish him Godspeed. Grandpapa had a hundred things to see to before he could go away. Little Wash rode one last time at his side when he went to inspect the farms.

Finally the day came when Grandpapa must ride away in his chariot. With him went Mr. Thomson and Grandpapa's old friend Colonel Humphreys. Tobias Lear had already journeyed to New York to prepare a home for the family. And Little Wash knew that there would be no more lessons in the tiny schoolhouse in the garden.

Now there were more exciting things to think of. First, Nelly and Wash must have clothes for their life

in the city. Needles flew from morn till night. There were a dozen new frocks for Nelly, of dimity and muslin, all trimmed with ruffles and bows. And pretty new caps for her soft brown curls.

Little Wash must have new buckled shoes and breeches and coats of sturdy homespun. And best of all, for him, were a velvet suit with silver buttons and a tricorn hat. Nelly and Cousin Harriot giggled when he strutted before the mirror, showing off. But Wash didn't care. He was eight years old now, and he felt very grown up in his new clothes.

"It's just like Grandpapa's," he said proudly.

Then there were trunks and boxes to pack, and there was the agonizing problem of what to take and what to leave behind.

Nelly appeared with an old wooden doll and an armload of books. Little Wash brought down his box of bright pebbles, a play bow and arrow, and a coonskin hat.

Grandmother held up her hands in dismay. "Children, children! We can't take everything. There will be rocks aplenty in New York, Little Wash, and new toys for play."

But in time the trunks were packed. Little Wash had to sit on the lids and bounce up and down so they could be closed and strapped. Then he followed the trunks outside and watched with interest as the coachmen stowed them into the great carriage that stood ready before the house.

Grandmother had so much baggage there was scarcely room for the passengers! Besides her and the children there was her little maid Molly, and a young cousin was joining them. His name was Bob Lewis. Grandpapa had sent him to escort them on the long journey.

When they finally crawled into the carriage they found it crowded. Grandmother's sassy green parrot was in a cage on the floor, dangerously close to Little Wash's legs. Nelly's tiny pet dog looked for a place to curl up, then jumped into her lap.

"Everybody ready?" shouted Cousin Bob. He leaned out the window to signal the driver.

Little Wash looked out from the other side of the carriage. His friends on the plantation had all come to bid them farewell.

One of the workmen was there with the hounds on a leash. Cousin Harriot was there, too. They waved and shouted as the coachman flicked the reins, and the restless horses started to move.

"Good-bye, good-bye!" they cried.

"Good-bye," Nelly called back. "We'll come home again."

"We'll bring you presents from New York," shouted Little Wash.

Then they were off down the lane and through the wide gates. Faster and faster went the carriage until it rumbled onto the highway. And Little Wash looked back one last time to the green and flowering hills of Mount Vernon.

Little Wash enjoyed riding in the carriage. He liked the pounding beat of the horses' hooves on the rough dirt road. He liked to watch houses and trees leap behind them as the carriage rushed onward.

At first the scenes along the way were familiar, for Little Wash and Nelly had been over the road many times, visiting neighboring friends and attending Grandpapa's church at Pohick. And the very first night of the journey was spent with beloved relatives at a plantation near home.

But next day, on the long long road to Baltimore, the adventure began in earnest. The carriage was like a small house moving along the highway. Molly had brought a big box of sweet cakes. Smiling, she passed them around. Grandmother took out her knitting and settled comfortably back in her seat. And Cousin Bob, who was a fun-loving young man, started a game.

"Little Wash," he shouted. "I see something that begins with a *C*."

Little Wash looked swiftly about. "Cow!" he cried. Then he spied a strange sight in front of the

carriage. "And I see something that begins with *F*," he shouted.

He had spotted a group of laughing children at the side of the road. They were waving wildly, and one of them held a flag—red, white, and blue with a circle of stars.

"Long live the President's family," they called out as the carriage sped by. Little Wash stuck his head out the window and watched until the children were mere specks in the distance.

People had learned that the President's lady was coming, and now, at every farm and hamlet, they

came out to cheer her on. Children threw flowers into the carriage, and Nelly and Wash caught them and waved in response.

It wasn't all fun, of course. The roads were full of potholes from the spring thaws. Once, the carriage gave a mighty lurch, and Little Wash tumbled from his seat as they came to a stop.

"Mercy," said Grandmother, dropping a stitch. "What was that?"

Little Wash picked himself up, none the worse for the accident. He and Cousin Bob jumped down from the carriage to find that the whiffletree had snapped. There was a tiresome wait while repairs were made.

Late in the day the carriage had to be ferried across the Potomac. A storm had arisen, and the wind was so strong it rocked the carriage from side to side and tossed spray into it, drenching Grandmother's yarn.

"Oh, oh!" squealed Nelly in alarm. The parrot squawked. The dog yipped. And Little Wash held fast to the doorpost, fearing every second that they'd be dashed into the raging torrent.

But the ferryman knew what he was about. With help from Cousin Bob, he delivered them safely across the river. The horses were ferried across separately. Soon, hitched once more to the carriage, they were galloping down the road.

All at once Little Wash felt a distressing pang in his stomach. They had been on the road for many hours, and Molly's sweet cakes had long since been devoured.

"I'm hungry, Grandmother," he complained.

"So am I," declared Bob. "I could eat a whole mule by myself, including the ears."

Everyone laughed at that. And Grandmother gave her wet knitting a vigorous shake.

"We'll soon be in Baltimore," she said. "And we'll stop for the night at Mrs. Charles Carroll's house. She is a dear friend, and I'm sure she'll have something more tasty for us to eat than mules' ears!"

Grandmother was right. Little Wash found a number of surprises at the Carroll home. First he discovered a merry-eyed boy peering from behind the tall pillars of the porch.

As Wash climbed from the carriage the boy ran down the steps. "Hello," he called out. "I'm Charles. You're George Washington's boy, aren't you?"

Little Wash nodded. "I'm George Washington,

too—George Washington Custis," he said, standing straight. "We're going to New York to live with Grandpapa."

"I know," Charles said eagerly. "We've been waiting and waiting for you. Will you come with me, please?"

Little Wash looked at Grandmother. She smiled, and he ran after the friendly boy, up the steps and into the house.

Charles led him to a table covered with white

linen. And that was another wonderful surprise. On the table were platters of meat and bread and frosted cakes and fruit. In the center was a huge bowl of icy punch.

Grandmother came into the room, then, and the hungry travelers gathered about the table. Little Wash ate until he was stuffed.

No sooner had he put down his plate than Charles was tugging his arm. "I want to show you something," he said.

So while Grandmother and Nelly chatted with Mrs. Carroll, Wash ran off with Charles, who had a litter of small brown puppies to show him.

That night there was a reception for Grandmother, and Nelly and the boys were allowed to stay up late to watch from the stairway.

While a band serenaded her from the terrace, guests in long gowns and handsome uniforms came to bow before Grandmother's chair. She wore a plum-colored brocaded dress with a lace cap on her snow-white hair.

"Doesn't she look like a queen?" Nelly whispered.

Little Wash had to agree. He waved through the banisters, and Grandmother looked up and smiled.

The band was still playing a lively tune when Wash finally curled up in a big soft bed and closed his eyes. Next thing he knew it was morning. "Wake up, George Washington!" Charles laughed, shaking the bedpost. "There's corn pone and ham for breakfast. And your grandmother's ready to ride away without you!"

Wash jumped out of bed and dressed in a hurry. He was sorry to say good-bye to Charles. But once he was in the carriage, seated across from Grandmother, he was anxious to be on his way again.

The horses were full of spirit that morning and raced through the pine-scented Maryland woods. Over green hills and across wide valleys they sped. And past more villages than Little Wash could count.

Day after day they drove on. Sometimes the coachman stopped to change the horses and to let Grandmother and the children rest. And everywhere they went they were showered with kindness.

The biggest celebration was in Philadelphia. When they came within sight of the city's steeples, Little Wash spied a band of townspeople coming toward them, women in carriages and men on fine horses. "They're coming to meet us, Grandmother!" he cried.

One of the carriages stopped near them, and a lady with feathers in her tall headdress stepped down. "It's Mrs. Robert Morris," said Grandmother happily. "She's invited us to stay at her home."

Then Mrs. Morris took Grandmother and the children into her own carriage. And with the horseback riders leading the way and the carriages behind them, the visitors entered the tree-lined streets of the city.

Suddenly a cannon roared. Little Wash was so startled he almost tumbled from his seat.

BOOM. BOOM. It came again and again, and he began to count. "Three–four–five.... *Thirteen shots,* Grandmother," he shouted.

"That's for the thirteen states in the Union," declared Nelly importantly.

Little Wash ignored her. He was watching the people who lined the street. There were hundreds of them, and when the carriage passed they cheered and waved their banners. And all the bells in the city pealed out in jubilant welcome.

Little Wash stood up and stuck his head out the window. He waved until Grandmother pulled him back to his seat.

"Look, Little Wash," she said, pointing to a building with a tall tower. "That's the Statehouse where the Declaration of Independence was signed. Your Grandpapa has told you about it many times."

Wash sat forward in his seat. He wasn't always attentive when Mr. Lear gave lessons. But when Grandpapa told stories about the colonists and their brave fight for freedom, he listened and remembered.

Now he heard a great bell ringing from the tower of the Statehouse. BONG! BONG! BONG! The sound was almost deafening.

"That very bell was rung in 1776 when liberty was proclaimed," said Mrs. Morris above the din. "And it rang for General Washington when he came to Philadelphia on his way to New York to become President."

And now it was ringing for Grandmother. A thrill of pride went through Little Wash.

Little Wash was growing tired of the constant excitement and the endless hours of riding over bumpy roads. All he wanted now was to be with Grandpapa again.

"It won't be long, Little Wash," said Grandmother, as if reading his thoughts. "Soon we will reach Trenton, New Jersey. Then on to Elizabethtown and our new home in New York."

"I hope Grandpapa has it ready for us," said Nelly.

In Trenton, the travelers stayed at Liberty Hall, the home of Governor William Livingston. And next morning they crept wearily back into the carriage for one last ride.

That day, even the horses seemed to know the longing of their passengers, for they raced over the road ever faster and faster until at last the coachman pulled to a stop before a house in Elizabethtown. A tall familiar figure in a brown suit stood by the hitching post.

Little Wash saw him first. He was out of the carriage almost before the wheels stopped spinning. "Grandpapa!" he shouted, running toward him.

A wonderful smile broke over Grandpapa's face. He put his hand on Wash's shoulder and looked down at him. "Little Wash! I do believe you've grown an inch since I last saw you. Did you have a good journey?"

"Oh, yes," said Wash. "But I thought we'd never get here."

Now Nelly was running to Grandpapa, throwing herself into his arms for his kiss. And Grandmother came up behind her and stood quietly waiting.

"Dear, dear Patsy," said Grandpapa, looking beyond Nelly's dark curls. "I trust you're not too exhausted."

"Not anymore, Papa," said Grandmother. "But it was a long ten days on the road. Now we're anxious to cross over to New York and see our new home."

Grandpapa put Nelly aside and ruffled Wash's fair hair with a gentle hand. "It won't be like our beloved place at Mount Vernon," he said. "But Tobias and I have done our best to make it comfortable for you."

Grandmother put her hand on his arm. "I'm sure we will be happy there," she said serenely.

Then they all went into the house to rest and eat and change their dusty clothes before Grandpapa took them to New York.

Grandpapa had left Manhattan Island at five o'clock that morning to cross the bay to meet his family. He had come in the presidential barge. And when Little Wash saw it later that day he felt sure he must be dreaming.

The great barge was decorated with flying banners of red, white, and blue. The oars were manned by thirteen stout men, all masters of ships, all dressed in white uniforms and black fringed hats. It was a magnificent thing to see.

As Grandpapa led his family on board a band played "The President's March," and a group of important men stepped up to meet them. The men called Grandpapa "Your Excellency." And Little Wash bowed and shook hands.

It was a sunny afternoon, and the blue water billowed and sparkled as the barge pulled away from Elizabethtown Point. There were other vessels in the bay—colorful barges and ships with shining sails. And as Grandpapa's barge moved slowly toward the

mouth of the Kills, the vessels fell in line behind it in triumphal procession.

Little Wash was so excited he ran to the prow of the boat, wanting to see everything.

The coxswain, a tall man named Thomas Randall, let Wash stand at his side. He pointed out the sights along the way.

"Now we are coming into Upper Bay," Mr. Randall said, as the barge made a great sweep around a rocky point. "And there, my boy, far beyond, is the

Hudson River flowing out to the ocean."

"Oh, Mr. Randall, look, look!"

Little Wash, scarcely able to breathe, pointed to a school of fish in the water. It was now sundown, and the fish were leaping in and out of the rosy waves, having a glorious time.

Mr. Randall laughed. "That's a school of porpoises," he said. "Porpoises are friends to sailors. They play about ships and bring us good luck. It's a fine omen for our President," he added. "And for our nation."

On and on the strong men rowed the barge. And all along the way more and more ships joined the parade. It was getting quite dark now, and lights began to appear on the decks. Lanterns could be seen moving along the shores ahead.

"There's Governors Island, lad," said Mr. Randall, pointing off to the right. "And look over there to the

left. See? People have gathered to greet your coming."

When the barge finally passed between the islands, the sound of joyous singing floated across the water. It lifted the heart of Little Wash.

Now he could see the houses and steeples looming against the dark sky on Manhattan Island. And as the barge moved up to the wharf he saw a throng of people waiting there. Thousands of men, women, and children were milling around on the shore.

Little Wash ran to stand beside Grandpapa and Grandmother. When the barge docked he followed them up the steps. And at that moment the air seemed to explode. A wild cheer rose from the crowd. "God bless the President and his family," the people shouted. "Long live George Washington!"

From the Battery, farther along the shore, cannons roared a thirteen-gun salute. And all at once, from

somewhere beyond the excited crowd, a volley of silvery white skyrockets rose and curved into the dark heavens. Rockets for the President! Rockets for the President's lady and the children!

Little Wash looked up in wonder and followed their flight across the sky. Skyrockets for the President! He felt joy in his heart and enormous pride for Grandpapa. He was sure now that happy times lay ahead for him and Nelly in their new life as children of the President.

Then Grandpapa took Grandmother's arm in his and led her grandly through the crowd to her own carriage, which had been ferried across the bay.

She looked back over her shoulder to smile at Nelly and Little Wash. "Come, my children," she said. "Grandpapa will take us home."

More About Little Wash and His Family

1781 George Washington adopted his wife's two youngest grandchildren when their father died. Nelly was two years old. Little Wash was only six months old. Wash was a fatty, and he was at first nicknamed Tub. Nelly and Little Wash had two older sisters, Patsy and Eliza, who remained with their mother at a nearby plantation. Their mother married a second time, and the children had several half brothers and sisters.

1784 Grandpapa's friend, the Marquis de Lafayette, who had helped the colonists during the Revolutionary War, paid a visit to Mount Vernon. Throughout their friendship, Lafayette sent Grandpapa many gifts. Among these were a pack of great hounds, several Chinese pheasants, and the key to the Bastille. The Bastille was a famous prison in France.

1787 Grandpapa's niece Harriot Washington came to live at Mount Vernon to be a playmate for the children. She stayed for seven years. Grandpapa had twenty-two nieces and nephews whom he helped to advise and educate.

1789 On April 30 Grandpapa took the Oath of Office as first President of the United States at Federal Hall on Wall Street in New York. In May of that year Grandmother—whom Grandpapa fondly called Patsy—arrived in New York with Nelly and Wash to live in the "presidential palace" on Cherry Street. At a grand reception a lady guest caught her feathered hat in a flaming candelabra. A gentleman present jumped to her rescue and put out the fire.

1790 The United States Government moved to the city of Philadelphia. Here Little Wash and Nelly spent six of the happiest years of their lives. In 1790 the family returned to Mount Vernon for a summer vacation and a reunion with Eliza and Patsy.

1793 Grandpapa was elected for a second term as President. On September 18 he laid the cornerstone for the capitol building in Washington, D.C. Little Wash and Nelly were present at the ceremony.

1797 An all-day celebration was held in honor of Grandpapa's birthday on February 22. There were 1,200 guests at his "birthnight ball." Grandpapa had refused to run for a third term as President, and at last the family returned to their beloved home at Mount Vernon.

1799 On February 22 Nelly Custis married Grandpapa's nephew Lawrence Lewis at Mount Vernon. Grandpapa wore his old blue and buff army uniform. On

November 27 Nelly's first child, a daughter, was born. And on December 14 Grandpapa died. He was buried in the family tomb at Mount Vernon. Around his neck was placed a locket containing Grandmother's picture.

1802 Grandmother died. She was buried beside her husband, and around her neck was a chain with a miniature painting of Grandpapa.

1804 Little Wash was married to Mary Lee Fitzhugh. They had several children, but only one lived to grow up. Her name was Mary, and she became the wife of Robert E. Lee, the famous Southern general of the Civil War. Little Wash lived on a plantation called Arlington. He painted pictures and wrote plays. He also wrote about Grandpapa. His writings can be read in a book called *Recollections and Private Memoirs of Washington*.

1824 Grandpapa's famous friend the Marquis de Lafayette and the Marquis' son, who was named after Grandpapa, visited America. They visited Nelly and her family at Woodlawn Plantation and Little Wash at Arlington.

1852 Wash's sister Nelly Lewis died. She left several grandchildren, and many of her descendants live in America today.

1857 Little Wash died. He was seventy-six years old.

1860 The Mount Vernon Ladies' Association of the Union took charge of the Washington home in Virginia. They turned it into a national shrine. The old buildings were restored. Some of the furniture was brought back to it. Today, Mount Vernon is almost as it was when Little Wash and Nelly lived there. Thousands of people visit it every year.

1864 During the Civil War, Little Wash's plantation was taken over by the government and turned into a national cemetery for war heroes. It is still called Arlington, and the Tomb of the Unknown Soldiers is there. But the very first graves at Arlington were those of Little Wash and his wife, Mary. Above them lies the home they built, now called the Custis-Lee Mansion. It, too, has become a national shrine and is visited by thousands of people from all over the world.

1976 The United States of America celebrates its Two Hundredth Birthday on the Fourth of July.

PRINTED IN U.S.A.

About the Author

Florence Laughlin cannot remember a time when she did not want to be a writer. "When my mother worked," she says, "I was left to look after my younger brother and sister and would entertain them with wildly imagined tales about a character named Big Red and an inexhaustible soup kettle." Though her literary style has surely matured, Mrs. Laughlin still carries on in her role as storyteller. Now an established author of children's books and grandmother of three, she occasionally gives talks at book fairs and writers' conferences and to children's story groups.

Researching *Skyrockets For The President,* Mrs. Laughlin discovered the warm and gentle side of the nation's first president. She saw him not only as a formidable public figure, but as a family man. "In *Skyrockets For The President,*" she says, "I have tried to give children a glimpse of this other George Washington through the eyes of his adopted son, Little Wash. It is a true incident in history about a great moment in both their lives."